Ajanta's Ledge

Poems

Ajanta's Ledge

Poems

SASCHA FEINSTEIN

The Sheep Meadow Press
Rhinebeck, New York

Designed and typeset by The Sheep Meadow Press. Distributed by The University Press of New England.

All inquiries and permission requests should be addressed to the publisher:

The Sheep Meadow Press
PO Box 84
Rhinebeck, NY 12572

Library of Congress Cataloging-in-Publication Data

Feinstein, Sascha, 1963 -
Ajanta's Ledge: poems/ Sascha Feinstein.
p. cm.
Includes bibliographical references and index.
ISBN 978-1-937679-08-8
I. Title.
PS 3556.E435A73 2012
811'.54 - dc23

2012034705

Acknowledgments

These poems first appeared in the following publications:

American Literary Review, "Ajanta's Ledge" and "Song for My Father."

American Poetry Review, "Everything Happens to Me, 1965."

Antietam Review, "Hanging Gardens."

Artful Dodge, "Poseur."

Blues for Bill: A Tribute to William Matthews, "Matthews in Smoke."

Crab Orchard Review, "Licorice Stick," "Plutonium," "Smalls' Paradise, 1929," "Town Outcast," and "When the Sun Comes Out."

88: A Journal of Contemporary American Poetry, "The Child Trees."

The Georgia Review, "Blues Sestina for Hayden Carruth."

Harpur Palate, "Anniversary Poem."

The Louisville Review, "Ascension."

The Missouri Review, "Lust Letters," "Night & Day," "Recovery Mission," "Shook Up," and "Swedish Sleds."

The New York Quarterly, "A was an Artist."

Nightsun, "After You've Gone."

North American Review, "The Taj."

Painted Bride Quarterly, "Crops."

Poetry Southeast, "Divia's Response."

Poets Against the War, "Blue Herons."
Solo Café, "Black Snapper" and "Cocktail Pianist."
West Branch, "Feels Like Burning Eggs."

"Plutonium" was reprinted in *Narrative* magazine.
"Song for My Father" was reprinted in *Palpable Clock: 25 Years of Mulberry Poets.*

Some poems were written with the aid of a poetry fellowship from the Pennsylvania Council on the Arts.

I am indebted to Stanley Moss, who made this a much stronger book, as well as David Jauss, Yusef Komunyakaa, and Robert Pinsky.

for Marleni, Kiran & Divia

We must admit there will be music despite everything.

—Jack Gilbert

CONTENTS

I.

II.

III.

I

Smalls' Paradise, 1929

The only things that the United States has given to the
world are skyscrapers, jazz, and cocktails. That is all.

—F.G.L.

You'd be right to imagine Lorca
    challenging the Gramophone's needle
        skittering across the 78:
    Lorca leaping to Ellington,
"Black and Tan Fantasy."

When he arrives in Manhattan,
    how can we not picture him
        dancing with the dancers?
    You'd be right to love his love
of Spanish passion, now giving into

Charlie Johnson's Paradise Band
    at Smalls', windowless and surreal
        on 2294 1/2 Seventh Ave.,
    just a block and a basement from
the Cotton Club's majesty and glitz.

Beneath the streets, the tables
    rock and rattle to George Stafford's snare,
        to Braque-like trumpet lines—
    Sidney De Paris battling Jabbo Smith.
Spotlit saxophones. "Wild Man Blues"!

It's easy—isn't it?—to admire
    Federico at thirty-one,
        slicked hair and tailored suit,
    shirt unbuttoned beneath his chin
as he spins a black woman

he'll later describe as an African exile:
I protested to see so much
flesh stolen from paradise.
Oh, the immigrants' cultural
compromise . . . But for now,

what joy to be at the center
of this gorgeous, fluid world.
El mundo ondulando . . .
You'd be right to imagine all that,
though you'd be exactly wrong.

To be true to history,
hypnotize his blazing spirit,
lower his head, place his arms
at his side, close his eyes,
have him whisper, *El ritmo . . .*

Let him wander while he sits
silently lost in the jazz club's landscape
where leopards purr and curl,
where the moon broods in the wet bell
of a trombone's metallic throat.

After You've Gone

—for 64842

They forged my horn in '25,
these craftsmen I'll never know
who sweated evenings by fires
that blazed their busy town

into the topographical map
of American music: Elkhart,
Indiana. This soprano sax,
a "low pitch" Martin,

changed hands how many times
in the fifty-five years before
my father and his two brothers
purchased the saxophone

for me? It's not that I desire
to live in Yeats' Byzantine dream,
reborn as a golden bell fashioned
to keep a drowsy audience awake,

but today I'm whistling tunes
I'm sure the artisans hummed
while they steadied their hands
to imprint this dazzling filigree

and the final brand: a serial number
to remind each generation
how many musicians
the horn outlives.

Blues Sestina for Hayden Carruth

Red house, red barn, mailbox. I'm not late
but I am, in most ways, unprepared to meet you,
lost in your own smoke beside the wood
stove. Slow rise, gentle hand. You brew
coffee. I set up the tiny tape recorder.
Your wife gives your shoulders a "Be good"
kind of squeeze, and then she's good
enough to let us be.
                                    I'm worried the percolator
will hiss-out the interview, that I'll only record
the ambience of your home and lose you
to the LP in the study, "Drunken Hearted Man" blues—

    My father died and left me
       my poor mother done the best she could.
    My father died and left me
       my poor mother done the best she could.
    Every man likes that game you call love
       but it don't mean no man no good—

those thirteen cuts from Johnson's blues
sessions in Dallas, '37, late
June—

    Tell me, milk cow
       what on Earth is wrong with you?
    Your calf is hungry—

                    the recordings
of "Hell Hound," "Love in Vain," the final recordings
of his life.

I begin with the obvious: "Could
you talk about freedom in poetry and jazz?" and you,
as if the question or answer could do any good:
"I have always tried to emulate
the improvisation that occurs, say, within a twelve bar blues."

And when I ask you more about the blues
you walk me to your wall of records,
the stereo covered in cat hair. I follow a slate
path out the pipe-smoked window that could
lead to Robert Johnson or God
knows where:

> Tell me, milk cow,
>   what on Earth is wrong with you?
> Oooooooo, milk cow,
>   what on Earth is wrong with you?
> Now, you have a little calf,
>   and your milk is turnin' blue.

I persist: "You once wrote about really good
jazz musicians—" [Carruth puts on a record]—
"'it would be worth / Dying, if it could
be done, / to be there with them.'"
                            But by now it's late
afternoon, and you're gone, your mind rerecording
the '40s, all those blues clubs where you could
punish grief just by arriving good and late.

Matthews in Smoke

All the better that he can walk
from his narrow apartment to the club
now called Smoke, then Augie's,
half the room on bar stools beneath
an olive-green mural of alcoholics
so polymorphically depressing
Bill *has* to respond: "Professors Emeritus."
We're in a neighborhood of trouble—
I'm ducking an old girlfriend,
he's ducking a new one—
so when the dour waitress returns
with bad wine and cheap Scotch
we skip a toast that would translate to
"Good night, night." We're here
mainly out of convenience, so
it's something of a shock when
a chunky tenor player from Chicago—
just twenty-one—saturates the room
with a thick, wet, Dexter Gordon tone.
In two years, he'll be known
(second place in the Monk contest,
the best near-win in jazz history)
but now he's swinging "Bewitched"
as a *waltz*, the lyrics—"I'm wild
again, beguiled again"—spun in thirds
across the high hat's steady shimmer.
The kid's making notice, and Bill forsakes
witty references, unveiled allusions,
triumphant alliterative punch lines—
he leaves them all in the bar's tip gutter.
Tonight, it's the real thing, music
putting language not to shame, exactly,
nor in its place. Tonight, language
burns faster than Bill's cigarettes.
Tonight it's all "Holy shit" and "Oh yeah."

Song for My Father

I. Duende

Had they been written, the words my father spoke
would not have filled a page, the loss of blood
addling, as though he'd suffered a stroke:

desire betrayed by unformed sound.
When my father slept, I tried to read,
though mainly I stood by his window,

the tenth floor of Mount Sinai overlooking
Central Park in full bloom. One afternoon,
a helicopter dragged a giant flag

above apartments and St. John the Divine,
above the wet and sunlit maple groves.
The pane of glass began to hum.

The flag had blessed Manhattan—
from the dismantled southern end on
up—to mark the final day of excavation.

When my father woke, his eyes focused on
a book in my hands. I tried to appear
hopeful. *Lorca*, I said. *A new biography,*

and he found a way to whisper, *Green . . .*
I heard each word: *how I want you   green.*

II. Fermata

Northway Road divides this morning
so unnaturally I almost stop driving

to stand on parallel yellow lines. Even
September trees separate:

evergreens out-muscling the oaks
freckled in their seasonal decay.

My father has been dying
for weeks now, his memory split between

a pellucid past, a vague present—
and suddenly I'm far too conscious of

metaphor, and try to lose myself
in milky farmlands and forests,

tufts of clouds and evaporating mist,
all that remains of house-rattling

thunder that woke my daughter
from the sleep reserved for children.

In the center of my vision,
I am steadied by a God-like moon

fully exposed in a swath of daylight,
unable to burn off the unyielding fog

nor burn itself from this paternal sky.

III. Louisiana, Denmark

Manhattan in January,
    too cold even to glance
        into any pair of eyes
as we exit the Strand
    where I've purchased
        a museum catalog:
Louisiana, Denmark,
    a place name as unreal as
        the legs of Walking Man,
stepping across continents.
    It's a gift, I suspect,
        more for me. We're all
in Giacometti's City Square,
    thin gray strangers
        momentarily caught
ambling across steel ground
    as if walking could define
        some magnificent effort
for each limited stride.
    Conceptualizing
        Giacometti's vision
beyond the nature of his art,
    I'm trapped in weighted shoes
        while memory recasts
a Danish sculpture garden,
    one extended, sunlit afternoon . . .
        How easy, this return,
even as I'm failing
    to age almost fifty years—
        my father's eighty-eighth
and last birthday—to know not
    what he needs
        but what he desires.

IV. Brief Elegy

As though your rhododendron could reclaim its bloom
from this spring that has never been spring, the rain
so unrelenting today I'm astonished by the sun,

or that the heart could recirculate the blood
no longer pulsing in your hands
beneath your still-warm face,

your towering canvas in the adjacent room
unveils a vibrant sky, a human pulse,
and the pulse of where you've gone.

When the Sun Comes Out

—for Eddie Green and Sonny Criss

You're bored with Singapore,
   with this ain't-close-to-bein'
      Philadelphia nightclub:

bamboo chairs and mirrors, pristine
   ventilation. It's "Satin Doll" and
      "Satin Doll" again. Your face

each ninety-degree afternoon
   turns a local eyebrow as you stare
      at skyscrapers, flamed glass

above smoldering satay grills,
   and you're lost in the summer of '68,
      the sweat of a New York studio

where you cut wax for Sonny Criss:
   Rockin' in Rhythm on the junkie label.
      It's July 2nd, and on the corner

of Broadway and 47th
   Doomsday Duane hollers
      death dates, Earhart and Hemingway.

You know there's talk of gun control,
   and what do you care? The *Times*:
      Ray extradited from London where

The Beatles top the charts.
   You stop at the white studio door.
      Sonny smokes in the corner,

shivers in heat, says, "Hey," then,
    "You'll shoot that piano," and
        then, chin to collar, whispers,

"Goddam producer's daughter, man—
    we're playin' 'Eleanor Rigby.'"
        Cranshaw and Dawson,

like clocks on a Monday,
    slog through a blues.
        Then Sonny calls for

"When the Sun Comes Out,"
    like he's asking for judgment
        and don't care for response.

Your intro descends into time,
    then you feather chords
        beneath his pleading saxophone.

Humidity seeps into the keyboard
    and you could be in Brazil
        where they're filming *Black*

Orpheus, overdubbing Jobim
    while boys just young enough
        to dance into belief

pull the sun to morning
    with solo guitar and samba.

Plutonium

Shimmering Selmers in the window, Sabrett
umbrellas on the corner, purpled Henrietta
boogie-jumping with her silver-haired studcake.

I'd gone downtown to buy a box of Rico 4s,
a half-step tougher than I could handle,
but what kid who's just bombed a chem test doesn't need

to blow a tenor with a stiff reed? Girlfriends
came later, and, oh, how I wanted just to *like*
chemistry, because my teacher hailed from Georgia,

wore sweaters that made little Jerry Steinbach
drop four beakers in three days. How he passed
I'll never know. Me? An extra-credit term paper:

"There's No Business Like Mole Business."
She loved me, but I learned nothing, nothing
except an olive-drab sense of failure that discolored

every incomprehensible question, not one of which
I can tell you now—but I remember the subway ride
home, bypassing the usual stop, heading straight for

my hole-in-the-wall, second-floor walk-up,
ordering Rico 4s with as much attitude as I had in me,
running my fingers across the waxy logo

to convince myself that, if I practiced long enough,
hard enough, if the yuppies in the apartment next door
didn't bang on the plaster like they always did

when I blasted *Tenor Madness*, shared a chorus or two,
maybe I could rub off depression like polishing silver.
I pocketed the reeds, then turned—*oof*—

into the belly of a giant clutching his black
sax case. Goatee and formerly-Mohawked skull.
Saxophone Colossus: Sonny Rollins.

He set his tenor on the glass case. *Check this out, Rod.*
Solid gold. Yamaha. A present from the Japanese.
Then, *Let me see your two best Mark VIs.*

Repairmen stopped banging out dents. I leaned forward.
And though Rollins didn't nod or say, *Hey there, kid,*
he must've known, as he pushed his own mouthpiece

onto the neck, I had daydreamed his solos
until chalkboards became bass and bass drum,
that gray slate of a propulsive rhythm section.

He must have known, and dismissed it. This wasn't about
me. It was about action and sound, a test
drive that started with fourths, then pentatonic scales.

Bitonal, quadritonal, heptatonic arpeggios.
Overtones became chords, an intervallic series to
mirror interval progressions. Palindromic canons.

Ditone progressions that turned into themselves
like mercury. Minor sevenths: aluminum, beryllium,
then a nickel-plated series of triplets. Magnesium

and manganese registers. Uranium C sharps that
rattled the store's neon and countertops.
And though he left without buying a horn—

having walked in, I think, just to show off his gold—
I knew I'd just heard triple-tongued
the whole goddamn periodic table.

Everything Happens to Me, 1965

i. Cannonball Adderley at the Capitol Recording
   Studio, New York City

   I can appreciate what you're saying,
and I know Bird got a lot of heat

for his string sessions. I've come to accept
   ignorance—no offense. My playing's

   not intended to please, necessarily.
As I said in the notes for the album:

This is simply one assault upon
   the tyranny of style, 'cause tyranny

fuels this LP. *Domination.*
   Consider that title, you dig? Reread
      what I've written. There's nothing technical

'bout my comments on these compositions:
   The tyrant will probably turn out to be
      music itself . . . which dominates us all.

ii. Marion Brown at *The Star Ledger* Offices, Newark

My best year, yeah. I've been in the studio
a lot. But I don't *sing.* (Listen, my brother—

if you're gonna cut the white reporters,
    do your homework. What'd your boss tell you?

That I was a woman?) [Laughs.] I just made
a quartet album—my first as leader.

Recorded with Trane earlier this year—.
    What's that? C—O—L—T—R—A—N—E . . .

Archie Shepp's *Fire Music*: that was *very*
    intense. We played "Malcolm, Semper Malcolm"
        as "Funeral"—for Evers. Medgar Evers.

It was the middle of February.
    We sure felt it . . . Then they wasted Brother Malcolm,
        though that was five long days later.

iii. Ornette Coleman on the Ferry from Denmark to
     Sweden

   Let me get this right. Forward to the border.
Stop. Cars detach. Half the train backs out. Tracks lock,

and then the front cars—with us—cross the dock
   into the ferry. That right? And we order

   food on the boat? Very cool . . . Now, tomorrow—
what's the place called? Golden Circle?—we play

nothing from last night's gig in Tivoli:
   "Lonely Woman," "Falling Star"—out. Only new

compositions. A kind of call and response
   to *all* of this: "European Echoes."
      "Faces and Places." "Snowflakes and Sunshine."

Train brakes on train tracks spiked to the deck. *Sounds.*
   We'll play travel *and* the moment, you know?
      "The Riddle": How does a boat swallow a train?

iv. Sonny Criss at Shelly's Manne Hole, Hollywood

Next day, I got all these telephone calls—
You okay? You see all that shit last night?

Watts . . . Never would have imagined it.
　　It's like I explained to Hampton Hawes:

I saw the flames, grabbed a fifth of J&B,
a folding chair, took 'em out to the lawn,

got comfortable. Felt like Nero! By dawn
　　the sky was all speckled in a blackish green

like, I don't know—like Bessie's blues,
　　or the cargo hold of some terrible slave
　　　　ship. But it was funny, too. What a sight . . .

I just recorded with Hawes back in June:
　　"When Sunny Gets Blue." "The Masquerade
　　　　Is Over." Boy, did we get *that* right.

v. Paul Desmond in Benjamin's Tavern, Stratford,
   Ontario

   So you can argue a dry martini
can't *sound* like a horn, that it has more edge

than my sound. Actually, I've come to regret
   the line itself—but not dry martinis!

   Just last week, in Brussels, Dave called for "Blue
Rondo a la Turk," and Morello limped

toward the stand, but I just couldn't
   leave that bar: Belgian blonde, late afternoon . . .

That first sip makes any gal your greatest date.
   Imperfections vanish like "My Funny
      Valentine"—the changes from the bridge on out.

Of course, by your fifth it's too late:
   your funny valentine has not only
      changed a hair for you, she's totally wigged out.

vi. Eric Dolphy (1928–1964) in Charles Mingus's
    Dream, Manhattan

  It's all sugar here: sugar clouds, sugar
women. You can taste your mouthpiece, Charles.

Sit at that black Formica table while
  I pour sugar from my palm. Can you hear

  the dancing grains? Think of a winter
ice storm, except it's the end of June

and you're lost in the streets of Berlin.
  When the sugar loses sound, you enter,

very softly, as though fingering patterns
  in this sweet sand. And now, the melody:
    D minor seventh, then a sudden leap—

Mingus, humming Dolphy's dreamsong, turns
  on his back, yells, *Eric, wait!—I'm not ready,*
    then, *Sue. Wake up. You gotta get me back to sleep.*

vii. Lee Konitz at Johanneshov Isstadium, Stockholm

Of course it's great to play with Bill Evans,
and, yeah, I'm sure he's still grieving. I mean,

when someone's so gifted and young—Scottie
    just made twenty-five—and he's your left hand,

    and then he's gone in a crash, you question
if you'll ever sound right again, if you'll

be a soul without a soul mate. Life's cruel . . .
    But what about *this* bass player. Exceptional

timing. Trust me if you can't hear it: this Dane's
    beautiful. Understand? You've got to feel
        the present and think of the future. This kid's

nineteen, for Christ's sake. Write down his name:
    Niels-Henning Ørsted Pedersen . . . Hey Bill,
        what do you call an O with a slash through it?

viii. Charlie Mariano at the Berklee School of Music,
    Boston

   That was February—two days after
the assassination of Malcolm X.

I was the only white guy there. My sax
    felt three times as heavy. Maybe four.

   But Elvin and Hank, Richard and Roland—
they said nothing. It was all about our

music . . . Toshiko and our daughter—
    we named her Monday—they're still in Japan.

She's about to record some of my tunes.
    Big band. The horn section's all Japanese:
        Shigeo Suzuki. "Sleepy" Matsumoto.

They shouldn't have much trouble laying down
    the charts. Can't speak for the rest. I mean,
        there's a chasm between technique and soul.

ix. Jackie McLean in Rudy Van Gelder's Studio,
   Englewood Cliffs

No, no, no, no, *no.* Four bars, ten beats—
everybody in unison—horns, drums,

everybody—and *then* the pickup.
   Here, bracket those bars—two sets of quintuplets.

What? Look, it's not one . . . It's not one . . . Jack!
Tell Larry and Larry to shut up. *Man* . . .

It's not one person's *fault.* You all got that?
   Okay? We'll just do another damn take.

(The Man's gonna take everything anyway,
   right? You're fighting like you're fighting for *justice*
      instead of focusing on the matter

at hand: *this composition.* Right?) Okay.
   Quiet . . . "Jacknife." Take *eleven* . . . Jesus,
      Charles. Why'd you write such a motherfucker?

x. Art Pepper in the Exercise Yard of San Quentin
   State Prison

   Stupid goddam parole violation.
That's all—or at least the most of it.

I was at a local club, my first gig
   after getting out. Felt real edgy. Then

   a waitress leans down and says, "There's fuzz
in this place," and then I see them staring

into my horn . . . "Everything Happens to Me"—
   You know the tune? [Sings:] *Your answer was*

"Good-bye," and there was even postage due . . .
   We played that beautifully. Long set, no breaks—
      I think we played for almost two hours

without a single break—but I knew
   they'd wait me out, so finally I said, "Thanks,"
      and stepped off the stand, into the applause.

II

Shook Up

Something about his ambivalence,
how he sluggishly relinquished his limbs
into the rowboat to search for his missing
wife. I was eight. What did I know of marriage

or murder, though a year later, a local
said I was right, told my mother no bay current
could force a body beneath a rock,
not like that, at least. But he got off.

If my parents were still alive, perhaps
they'd remember more, though it hardly matters.
A man dove with his wife, bear-hugged her,
knocked the oxygen from her mouth till she drowned,

then wedged her body so it might appear
she snagged her leg and panicked. *Shook up,*
the lifeguard said when I told her he did it.
You should have seen when he first came to shore.

Denial

Black Snapper

As a child, I fell into the minnows
glinting across frog eggs, and now, as
my own children cross precarious rock,
I offer parental warnings I grew up

disregarding. My son spies a snapping turtle,
asks me to yell when it breaks the surface,
then runs with his sister toward heron nests,
beyond paths now sealed in poison ivy

where I used to venture to view
Brewster's grist mill waving to the Atlantic.
Those paths are off limits now, but still
I ask my kids to stop by the wooden bridge

to maintain the unobscured panorama,
so they can hear me call to them
when the submerged black snapper
shatters the past with its ancient, bony head.

Patience/Tradition

Water Lizard

Almost goose-like in its arc above
the pond's reflective finish, the water
lizard barely disturbed wild grass
and lily pads shirring in warm rain.

Years ago, elsewhere in Indonesia,
my guide swerved his Jeep, cheered as he crushed
something similar, a gator-like reptile
he claimed ate chickens. It was good to kill

all of them, he said, as though they were roaches,
though I knew a woman who lived amid
ectoplasm and droppings, unable
to set traps or bombs for primordial

scavengers scuttling throughout her apartment.
Where do we draw the line? Alligator-
serpent, temporary keeper of this pond,
whatever your descent: swim away from us.

Hierarchy

White Noise

I believe I woke because of silence,
the absence of heaters and expanding woodwork,
of truckers rattling through town, or hillside trains.
Not even a child whispering to a dream

down the hall where faint calls still slip
beneath our bedroom door. Knowing
the insomniac's clock too well, I waited for
song-less cardinals in the frosted holly.

Then wind from the Susquehanna
unleashed a tree's worth of prickly leaves
from the lawn to the house's wide grin—
bricks of teeth and shuttered eyes—

like a circus finale when a man in tights
outlines the suspecting beauty queen
with curved Egyptian knives, or the flickering
television in your anxiety dream.

Beauty of the insignificant

Town Outcast

Each mole across her neckline—dead stars
oscillating a ravished moon—spins
retrograde as she catches passing stares
as though she'd washed up on shore. She still lives

among the grown school girls who teased her
more viciously than boys tormenting locusts.
Her past's a sand flat of memory:
half-buried mollusks and mussels.

For thirty years, she's grown into a face
swollen like bread in water, ambulatory
as guilt. She'll outlive them all. Each Sunday,
she hears young mothers in the Chinese wet market

mouth her name as though whispering
Cancer—the nebulous disease,
not the sign of the crab, digging mud holes
in response to the dictatorial moon.

Asbestos Removal

The Asbestos Boys have arrived!
Silver-suited and factory sealed,
they position multi-bladed fans
to jettison airborne particles

out of my basement, onto my lawn.
(Take that, crab-grass. I'm cleaning house.)
Hours later, surveying gleaming pipes,
the team's chain-smoking foreman will admit,

You were never in any danger.
He'll hand me a poisonous bill, and I'll ask,
Is that asbestos you can do? Tough room . . .
But for now, they're on the clock,

vacuum-packed and basting like turkeys
in oven bags, pouches sizzling with sweat,
misery's industrial insulation,
defying the boiling points of body and soul.

Night & Day

Say the whole day could be Count Basie,
so you leap out of bed already dressed
in what Singaporeans call "casual chic,"
get pumped up on pancakes and coffee

already *made*, right?—because, of course,
you have millions, and are in love,
and she loves you (get this) for your *mind*.
Out the door, arm around her waist,

and suddenly you know how to dance
meringue, you're a star being filmed while
gondolas glisten overhead, releasing
mile-long, sherbet-colored ribbons. Yes . . .

and every three or four minutes, the day's
eclipsed—that necessary pause between
tunes—before the arrival of the sun,
warming the earth with its time-delayed light.

Licorice Stick

You've forgotten you've forgotten
the lower register of the clarinet,
forgotten the glitzy drunk of gin,
martinis with a twist of bad fingering—

but forget all that. Here's the moment
the smell of cork grease intoxicates ego,
when the chilled silver bullet brightens
tarnished keys. The sweetness of vermouth

blurs the blues into something recognizable,
though not memorable. You'll never be
Pee Wee Russell playing "Mariooch,"
plastered but brilliant, his *sotto voce* solo

oleaginous as juniper-soaked olives.
For the time being, you're willing to live with
botched riffs as a familiar hint of
pimento tinctures your betrayed tongue.

Cocktail Pianist

Imagine the years of discipline,
the professor who rapped his knuckles
for each less-than-cheesy transition.
Tuxedo for graduation, goldfish-bowl

tip jar with free advice for seeding bills,
lengthy lists of soporific songs
no one will hear. He's tied a yellow ribbon
'round an old oak tree as well as

an old chestnut in blossom. April
in Paris, or summertime—who cares?
He's a stationary elevator
in which people wait while cabs get hailed,

while families pace in the lobby for
that fiery uncle late from the pub
where he's loaded the oldies jukebox
with tunes he thinks he can't live without.

The little things
in life

Urologist Encounter

I want to ask how many cock jokes he's endured
since most half-clever minds can unzip
any image, and surely this man always knows
what's coming. We've been introduced

and abandoned by a host who, as a child,
loved derailing toy trains and burning ants.
Someone's told the doc I like music
(punch line: Urethra Franklin), that I write

poetry (punch line: Wang Wei). He stands
like a man who's spent much too much time
peeping, yet I've shaken his hand. (Punch line:
James Dickey.) We're getting cocktails.

My pocketed fingers feel like criminals,
my Scotch suspiciously familiar
in color, on the rocks, belted down.
I have no follow-ups. We're different that way.

Awkward

Lust Letters

So these are the letters you yearned for,
the ones for which you pedaled like mad
to the post office, praying for smutty lines
or disgustingly wistful refrains.

Now they're nearly unbearable to read.
Rounded, scented lettering. SWAK on the flap.
But who's to say titillating pubescence
isn't necessary for marriage?

We convince ourselves we know what love is.
You might as well romp a bit, save the notes
in a sealed box, then forget the lot
for twenty years, say, when, suddenly,

you find them in your hot attic
and read just one—one is more than enough—
before throwing them in your neighbor's trash
and ambling home for dinner.

Recovery Mission

Homeless alien: paper-bag helmet, goggles,
fisherman's waders below a blue flannel shirt
no one would dare to wear in August. Gloves
streaked in mower fluid. Insecticide. Fly swatter

poised as he fumigated the bored hole.
We heard only the repetitive *whap* as dazed,
nearly immobilized, writhing wasps emerged
to be smacked and snapped, our concrete porch

pocked with cracked abdomens, stingers,
thoraxes. Then another hive's-worth descended
not on my father but on the dead, lifting remains
into the sky, the woods. When he stripped down

to shorts, bare-chested, he looked lost.
I asked if he was okay, if he'd been stung,
and he said he smelled honeysuckle
from someone's yard, very far away.

Ambitious

Swedish Sleds

Two boys slid down a hill and one crossed
a road that defined their small town by
the mere lack of traffic, a road twisting
through the bypass before plunging down-

country. People talked of the road for months
before it was built: less time to go North,
but who leaves anymore? Two boys slid down a hill,
and neither heard or saw the logging truck,

and the one who slid between the axles—
my uncle—grew up to praise luck, to fear
Scandinavian fate, Thor's fierce hammer,
that bolt of destiny executing

delirious youth. Sixty years later,
he can't quote his best friend's last words—
"I'll cross the road before you"—without
a shot of chilled aquavit.

III

Hanging Gardens

—for Eleni Larned

Maybe Welfleet's tide pools
   inspired that green for
      the sculpture I love, *Fog,*

those two wooden hands
   extending not just into
      the last room of your life

but here, outside Bombay,
   where I expected to experience
      everyone else's loss.

You would have snickered
   at this topiary garden,
      mocked every obvious shape,

the sprouting giraffes, leafy
   hippos. Talent isn't nature
      turned cleverly unnatural,

but this was part of the city
   tour, and strangely near
      the Tower of Silence

where Parsis leave their dead
   at the widening drive
      to be blessed and left behind.

No one except
   Nassesalars can witness
      the courtyard of corpses

splayed across stone wells,
   or the vultures
      catching the scent.

Bones and cartilage tumble
   to damp earth. Years ago,
      birds cooled themselves

in the wide reservoir, but they dropped
   skin and strips of muscle,
      so the king commanded

Hanging Gardens,
   bizarre greenery that cloaks
      the expanse of water.

"Where do the birds drink
   now?" is a question
      no one asks, as though

tongue-tied
   by tame, spiritless
      sculptures. Eleni,

I didn't even know
   you were ill, and maybe
      not knowing was best.

My vision of you—wry
   '50s-starlet smile,
      a chainsmoker's laugh

billowing wonderful
   Don't-fuck-with-me
      imperatives—sears

these phony leaves,
　　your voice from
　　　beyond the Tower:

What will getcha will getcha.
　Until then, make something
　　of this world.

A was an Artist

He never wanted me to dream fire,
to imagine steaming glue slowly unrolling
paisley carpet, stair by stair, banisters
sparking as they bent and extracted clutched spokes.

The samovar glowed, he said, before it buckled.
Fruiting trees of wallpaper flashed chemicals
as family portraits within heavy lead
branded black checkers across a lavish hall,

rising into the second floor study where
a new light consumed lampshades. Bookshelves
flamed silver quills, and then the pine esplanade
collapsed in a symphony of cinder. Upstairs, too,

the illustrated alphabet had burned page
by page, back to front, until a January draft
lifted the first letter's charred spine and released it
upon juniper above the hissing sleet.

A was an Artist. So unusual,
this painter in profile staring beyond
the vulnerable woodcut's singed edge.
I was old enough to know I'd have to grow

into this gift, but I thanked him
as my father locked the print in a bureau.
Then I said goodnight, left them to talk,
but from my bedroom one floor below,

my ear to the painted iron vent,
I heard them clearly, how this fire's ash
reclaimed ashes of memory—the encampment,
the wild smoke, the smell of flesh:

You would think, as we shivered,
I would contemplate the melting brass.
We wept—sure—as my cloth shirt
burned, the one I never washed,

the one that held both Morris brothers—
Don't cry . . .
What I mean to say is
we are born so many times.

He lived, my parents later explained,
only two more weeks. I never saw him again.
But as I write these words, his woodcut,
no more damaged in the thirty-five years

since its flight through smoke and winter,
marks time overhead in a gilded frame.
When I lean back, this one surviving page reads
like a challenge and a blessing.

Feels Like Burning Eggs

*I've spent my whole career learning how to paint
like a five year old.*

—George McNeil

When the mind moves like a child's
we embrace the *all* without
edits, without what we call a "mastery"

of language—or am I simply thinking of
that woman power-walking the cemetery?
Purple headphones, probably C & W

or humpbacks moaning.
Someone's stooped over a grave,
perhaps for a spouse, half a century of

love. Grief and glitter
nearly collide
like first speech.

What is it my son said
as we drove through a storm
to kindergarten, first day,

mausoleums awash in seedlings,
buckled traffic cones
bouncing from lane to lane?

The sound of the rain feels like burning eggs.

Divia's Response

The day my daughter asks
why airplanes fly

into buildings,
she shows me a drawing.

It has no name, she says.
It's just a painting.

The shaded part
is a moutain.

Beneath it,
a giant heart.

The mountain is a Mountain
of Doom, with spikes,

but the circles,
they're Dream Rivers.

Some Xs are volcanoes.
Some are camels.

The sand is made of gold.
The heart is made of sand.

Some of the camels
are sleeping.

Poseur

Produced by an affair of the spleen, you court
art, marry your teacher, insist you're above fame
though you're below quality's county line.
Realistically, you'll never attempt a self-portrait.
It's part fate that the person who outlines bodies in
chalk possesses more talent. Last week,
in the city where you were born, where,
as a poet once wrote, they know twenty-seven words for
snow, a glacial boulder loosed itself from sludge, denting
the city's landmark. Many hoped it was a meteor,
a cosmic awakening rather than an igneous rock
re-emerging as its own exquisitely dull self. It seemed
karmic, how every crushed flower peeled off and blew away.

Blue Herons

Against a window of unresolved
    Morning light, an unfinished
        Martini floats a lemon rind
Like a goldfish. Again, she's risen

Before five, muscles in her back
    Contracting for heat.
        "The cost," she'll tell me,
"Of wedging stoneware."

Tossed by someone never seen,
    The *Herald* hits her door with news
        She's avoiding—ground war—
So for now she leaves the paper

Tucked into itself, corks the merlot,
    Smooths the pillows—evidence
        Of her small divorce party.
From all-night wood firings,

Her body smells gray,
    "Seasoned," she likes to say,
        Smiling like her porcelain portraits:
Pre-Raphaelite lips, hair spiraling

Into grapevines and honeysuckle.
    On a milk pitcher: blue roses
        Within a matte ebony finish.
Touching those engraved petals,

I told her of a lagoon in the Yucatàn
    Where I held my breath to crawl
        Down a collage of basalt caverns,
How the walls pulsed and shimmered

As iridescent, indigo fish
   Emerged and withdrew
      Until I let go and rose,
Desperate as a flame for oxygen.

It's almost time
   To open the kiln, smoldering
      In the dawn's amber fog,
And her vision's spinning with possibility:

If the handful of rock salt
   Thrown in the ninth hour
      Exploded perfectly
Into a nebula of glaze,

If the goblets kept their shape,
   If the soup tureen's heavy lid
      Still settles within its rim.
She unfolds her newspaper to face

Part of her broken world:
   Static-stricken charts
      Of missiles navigating
Baghdad at midnight

And clotted Gulf shorelines,
   Those useless efforts
      To cleanse the feathers of
Blue herons paralyzed in oil.

Ascension
Singapore, 1999

My wife's family rushed
    the marketplace, *Mr. Wong*

    a stricken echo
amid the steaming woks,

fresh sea bass on ice,
    sizzling prawns in *mee*,

    the crates of restless chickens,
the throat-slit, hanging ducks.

Perhaps he had stopped
    to watch the fishball seller

    hypnotically palm red snapper,
its flesh scraped and pressed through

the crux of thumb and forefinger
    in a clench faster than sight:

    a perfect white globe
balanced momentarily on a fist.

I kept returning to the bridge,
    certain he had leapt, certain now

    he paused above passing cars
motoring to the inner city or Johor,

then envisioned the backseat
    with a child or a young lover.

    How to imagine the mind
of a stranger, a man

I knew only as
    a cancer-ridden neighbor

    mostly confined to a bedroom,
laboring to stand?

The year before, with pills
    collected beneath his pillow,

    tucked in a dry cheek,
undissolved, he swallowed

what he believed to be
    a fatal throatful, but

    they pumped his stomach
and brought him back.

And there we were,
    his maid having telephoned,

    hysterical Mandarin:
The old man has disappeared.

I remember walking
    from the overpass,

standing in the lot beneath
newly painted apartments

which, shortly before,
he entered like a ghost.

In those minutes when
the elevator slowly rose,

or when he reached
the common landing

where he dropped his cane,
caught his breath, raised

a leg over the low wall,
heaved his ribbed torso onto

the ledge—did he hear us
calling his name?

I did not witness the release
but I ran when I heard

his body hit the hard earth.
He had rolled

into a water drain, his face
skyward, his eyes wet and vague.

But it was terribly clear
he had not yet died.

I leaned over his body, whispered,
    Oh, Mr. Wong as his lips

    spasmed like a carp.
In those seconds of transition,

my sun-bleached face
    must have appeared

    to be a strange angel
uniting worlds.

The Taj

Like most "last breath" stories, this one's a good lie:
how Mumtaz Mahal, still bleeding from childbirth,

pulled Shah Jahan to her mouth, begged for
a temple in her memory. How he based the dome

on the curve of her breast. How, when she dies,
he turns gray overnight. We know she's entombed

twenty-two years later, that he's deposed
by his son and—every guide will tell you this—

imprisoned in Agra Fort so he'll die overlooking the Taj.
It's a death sentence, too, for the dream of a bridge

and a perfect shadow in black marble. Instead—
and this fact's true as death—he's buried

beside his wife, breaking absolute symmetry
for another form of perfection. Even in India,

our greatest love stories are never quite enough.

Anniversary Poem

From the stone tip of a carved mallet
drums coax a sun to its balance above

this floating palace in Jaipur, the one you touched
in picture books when family elders foretold

the rhythms of your future. What map
can I draw from this line of salt

outlining the rim of your collarbone,
and can it also be that drums tease the moon

so that these walls rise, the way you leaned into me
and then collapsed into Shiva's everlasting embrace?

When I taste the warmth of your throat
I could be water lost in water, I could be

a drum skin's hillside echo, I could be the man
who held you twenty years ago in a wedding suite,

aquamarine wallpaper. Lie back.
Dry yourself beneath the ceiling fan. Let me

lift from your shoulders your uncut hair
tangling beneath teak mythologies.

The Child Trees

I. 1974

Three fingers and, almost, a hand
from a swamp-colored sleeve
glide to the left, and then the form
stands—or at least makes the sound

of chair legs inched across a floor
by the back of someone's knee—
and he's reaching for a photograph.
When the TV frames his face, poisoned

boils, his nose a warted gourd,
perforated and swollen, I mouth the word
leprosy. My grandmother's carpet
pockmarks my elbows. New camera angle:

his wife in slow motion as she dusts
a pine tabletop with a yellow cloth perfect as
a manikin's wig. Through a window,
their cat, a surrogate son or daughter,

disappears. The whole frame begins to blur.
Her checkered apron, the hanging knives,
the glass of milk, the olive rug—
it's all an unnatural, muted sheen.

Even her legs discolor into
cabinets and cupboards, fumed
like chlorine. It's their first apartment,
and now the snapshot from the past:

her delineated lips, cheeks
full and mildly blushed,
and with his collapsing throat he says,
in Swedish, "Better days."

Hours later, near that colony's cemetery,
we carried torches up a hillside
warmed by enormous bonfires
until we reached what Uncle Jörgen called

The Child-Eating Tree,
the one that devours little boys
if they wander within a branch's grasp.
The crusted trunk consumed

the fence's iron spike, mouth to fork,
its bark bulging like amber.
My cousin's blind child
gripped the gnarled growth,

recoiled, slipped from our sight
vaporously, a spirit
among thickets of bayberries
ripening beneath the midnight sun.

How many years did that tree labor
to wet the flaking iron, to forever
hold its persistent, silent kiss?
That evening, a child ran

to what could have been
a slope of rock shards and pine needles
or a troll's shaded cave
where the moss is deep and thirsty.

Maybe his fall frightened the fox.
Maybe a trail of fire ants
coaxed the copperheads
to sleep within the earth.

When he bruised his fingers
on a massive gate, heard his sister weeping
in a semicircle of stone angels,
he knew we'd save him.

II. 1994

Afterwards, when I helped you into the car,
I wondered if we would even grieve.
Then your tears, and my slow drive

through what would become
a record snowfall, immobilizing
the city. You made one long call home.

I listened to Miles. We ordered in
for several days. No ceremony
for this miscarriage. No long reflections,

until today, the whole family down
with the flu, and I'm projecting
slides of Indonesia:

Sulawesi, Tana Toraja,
where the wealthiest bury their dead
in stone graves checkering basalt boulders,

their wooden effigies reaching toward
ancestral rice fields. Elsewhere:
a visual litany of corpses,

dangling femurs from rotting
earthen tombs, the skull-
and limb-ridden ground. But I had forgotten

that remote Baby Tree where mothers
carry what must be unbearable—
dead children wrapped in cotton cloths—

to place them upright within a Tarra tree,
carved graves concealed by thatched palm
until the trunk can heal itself. For years

the children ascend . . .
What member of the tribe
creates these living, wooden tombs?

How many years of apprenticeship
to pursue if not master
this ceremony of tragedy?

It must be art or alchemy
to know how much one can cut
without killing the tree itself.

Crops

Some seasons the family remembers:
that spring when Po Sen's mother
gave birth to her in a field that yielded
nothing and forced the women
to buy rice near a river village.
They hunched and pressed their foreheads
into cloth straps—*Like this*, she seems to say,
and places my hand on her thigh
so I can feel it turn to stone as she lifts
water jugs filled from the stream.
Some carried their babies
in sling bags across their bellies
as they climbed for seven hours,
sacks of rice fusing to their spines.

The next dry season, three daughters left
for the city American soldiers call
Paradise. No one here speaks of AIDS
or possible futures, and this year the first crop
failed, but Po Sen points to her father
handling their largest water buffalo's yoke,
and then to the wet sky. She's painted her face
with a lotion made of crushed bark
to make her skin delicate as the transient
rain, or this heavy mist. She peers beyond
the protective thatch as her mother plants
seedlings, palms open to the wind
and moving more quickly than the grain.

Ajanta's Ledge

—for Marleni

I.

The Waghora River channels July rain.
  It's off-season, and we're almost alone
    in our ascent to the pillared caves.

Horseshoe of basalt. Perfect curve below.
  Lost city at sunrise. When we enter
    the first sanctuary of murals,

Bodhisattva Padmapani, Bearer
  of the Lotus, leans beside a charcoal
    princess. It's our tenth anniversary

and a pilgrimage, perhaps, for my wife
  whose great-grandfather, when she was five, told
    lavish stories of these sixth-century

carvings, stories traveling like this light:
  thin weave of morning blue, morning gold.

II.

Heavy midnight-blue sari, gold weave
    across the border, shoulder to waist—
        and she's drenched, and laughing. When I see

        this new bride within a downpour, her face

        almost reflecting the relief of Ananda,
    I fall back ten years into my own marriage,
take my wife's hand. This woman's husband

seems dull as uncut rock, and their arranged
    marriage will last seven lifetimes—a myth,
        apparently, of pure joy. She could spin

        a dance of lapis, a cool blue fire

        between river valley and monolith.
    Maybe, beneath dripping silk, a new skin,
she knows everyone's decorated with desire.

III.

For someone's home décor, out of desire—
or was this commissioned?—the British

razored half-inch grooves into deserted
murals, these caves discovered by John Smith

during a tiger hunt. They angled buckets
to drip overnight, seeping behind mud,

the painters' base, until stiff pigments buckled
and squares of tempera peeled from each scored cut.

Queen Sivali still kneels, luminous pearls
following the curve of her full breasts—

she's begging the king not to leave the palace,
not to abandon the material world—

but on what wall, in what museum or locked chest
can you recover her stolen face?

IV.

If, eyes adjusting to Buddha's stone face
in the shrine of the seventeenth cave,
its chiaroscuro suggests a grimace,

you must follow the light throughout the day
as his lips rise into a veiled laugh,
and, in the hour of prayer, Serenity.

Now, a hired local carries an oil lamp:
amber glow, left, right, center, as if he
directed the sun, colored the hemisphere—

no, that's not what I mean to say. The shame's
not his, and not only Western, though Ajanta's
artists, the thousands who made nothing here

out of ego, could never have foreseen
the impatient heartbeat of America.

V.

We're beat, turn on CNN, America
in half an hour, and call room service,

Eagle beer and vegetable pakoras.
It's all footage we've seen: the Cessna's

flight plan, the salute from '63. Repeat
and fade. Only in passing do they mention

another search, Mount Rainier, and it's weeks
before, by chance, I learn the hiker's name:

Joe Wood, a high-school pal. Broken snow bridge,
they think. Inexperience. But they can't

find Joe's body. Besides, the news is all John-
John falling from the sky, and now the pilgrimage

to his apartment, cameras flashing to a chant,
city cops: "Say your prayers, and move on."

VI.

Cities and palaces. It's time to move on.
   Our driver's drinking tea to The Rascals,
      climbing the charts once again: "Movin'

      down a crowded avenue . . ." Soon we're stalled

      behind painted truck bumpers—*Horn Please Horn*—
   lost among bicycles, camels, rickshaws,
and then: fields of ruby and saffron

saris, and dancing peacocks, mating calls.
   Head to my shoulder, my wife's speaking
      in a dream, hieroglyphics of sound.

      When Sivali followed Bodhisattva

      into the forest, relinquishing
   his kingdom, how could he break the grass stalk,
leave her for a cave in the Himalayas?

VII.

I can't leave Ajanta, the many layers
    of story and stone, though I see myself,
        sometimes, as a mere surveyor of

this ancestral homeland for my wife.
    What deity arranges a marriage,
        selects soul mates for seven lifetimes?

How many years just to carve the ledge
    where we stopped to watch that blue, rainwater bride?
        Maybe, in ways I cannot, she can embrace

time and vision, can actually see
    decades of artists spreading mud and lime
        washed smooth for the murals' surface.

Belief is a road between will and destiny.
    You might as well challenge the rain.